who?

Mao Zedong

마오쩌둥

Biography Comic
who? 29 Mao Zedong

개정판 1쇄 인쇄 2014년 3월 5일
개정판 1쇄 발행 2014년 3월 10일

글 정현희
그림 스튜디오 청비
번역 채드 워커
감수 김수희
펴낸이 김선식

책임편집 이유미 **디자인** 박효영
콘텐츠개발팀장 김선영 **콘텐츠개발팀** 박효영, 이유미, 김선민, 조서인
마케팅본부 이상혁

펴낸곳 스튜디오 다산 **출판등록** 2013년 11월 1일 제414-81-37694
주소 경기도 파주시 회동길 37-14 3층
전화 02-702-1724(기획편집) 02-703-1725(마케팅) 02-704-1724(경영관리)
팩스 02-703-2219 **who클럽** cafe.naver.com/dasankids
종이 월드페이퍼(주) | **인쇄** (주)현문 | **제본** 광성문화사

ISBN 979-11-5639-021-3 (14740)

who?

Mao Zedong

마오쩌둥

글 정현희 | 그림 스튜디오 청비 | 번역 채드 워커 | 감수 김수희

Dasan Kid

Mao Zedong

Chinese politician, December 26, 1893 ~ September 9, 1976

The leader who established current day China, Mao Tse Tung, was born in 1893 in a town called Shaoshan in China's Hunan province. His father was a landowner in the village, so their family had enough means but his patriarchal father made him help out on the farm. As a result, Mao quit school after less than five years of schooling, and spent his childhood working on the farm.

During the peak of the revolution to tear down the decaying Qing dynasty , Mao participated in the Chinese revolution to take away the sovereign power of the king and establish a modern republic. Through this experience, he realized the value and importance of revolution. Mao then decided to bring about another revolution by introducing communism to create a new China.

As he gathered together farmers and laborers to resist the landowners by holding demonstrations, his position as a leader became solidified. However the landowners saw Mao Tse Tung's power rising and chased him out of power.

Mao led his supporters in a ten thousand kilometer journey called the "Long March." After successfully completing this extensive trek, the communist party put their faith in Mao, who then established a base by gathering all of the powers within the divided China in order to create a new nation.

He defeated the opposing powers and in 1949, he declared the establishment of the government of the People's Republic of China and worked hard to improve the nation as its chairman. Mao Tse Tung dreamed of a revolutionary society in which peasants were at the center. He implemented a movement called the "Great Leap Forward" to improve the national economy and established a strong central power system.

The majority of the reforms that Mao pushed for actually failed, but he is remembered by people all over the world as the powerful leader who created modern day China.

마오쩌둥

중국의 정치가, 1893년 12월 26일 ~ 1976년 9월 9일

현대 중국을 완성한 지도자 마오쩌둥은 1893년 중국 후난성의 사오산 마을에서 태어났습니다. 마을의 지주로서 넉넉한 생활을 했지만, 가부장적인 아버지 아래서 자란 그는 학교 공부를 5년도 채 하지 못하고 농사일을 하며 어린 시절을 보냈습니다.

부패한 청나라 왕조를 무너뜨리기 위한 혁명이 한창이던 당시, 마오쩌둥은 왕권을 빼앗고 현대적인 공화국을 수립하기 위한 신해혁명에 가담합니다. 그 일을 통해 혁명의 가치와 중요성을 깨달은 그는 공산주의 사상으로 혁명을 일으켜 새로운 중국을 세우기로 마음먹습니다.

그는 노동자와 농민들을 모아 부패한 관리와 지주들에 대항하는 시위를 벌이면서 지도자로서의 입지를 굳힙니다. 그러나 마오쩌둥의 세력이 커지는 것을 경계한 지주 세력들은 그를 몰아내려 하였습니다.

마오쩌둥은 자신을 지지하는 사람들을 이끌고 1만 킬로미터를 이동하는 '대장정'을 시작합니다. 이 긴 여정을 성공적으로 마치자 공산당에서는 그를 믿게 되었고, 마오쩌둥은 당원들을 이끌며 흩어진 중국 안의 세력들을 모아 새 나라를 세우기 위한 기반을 다집니다.

반대 세력과의 싸움에서 이기고, 1949년에 중화 인민 공화국 정부 수립을 선포한 그는 주석으로 취임하여 중국의 발전을 위해 힘씁니다. 혁명을 일으키며 농민이 중심이 되는 사회를 꿈꾸었던 마오쩌둥은 경제를 발전시키기 위해 '대약진 운동'을 실시하고, 강력한 중앙 집권 체제를 확립하였습니다.

그가 추진한 개혁은 대부분 실패로 돌아갔지만, 마오쩌둥은 오늘날까지 현대 중국을 이룬 강력한 군주로서 세계 사람들에게 기억되고 있습니다.

이 책을 만든 사람들

글 · 정현희

어린이들이 알고 싶고, 궁금해 하는 것들을 재미있는 만화로 알려 주는 데에 보람을 느끼는 작가입니다. 꿈을 포기하고 싶을 때마다 용기를 주었던 위인들을 생각하며 이 책의 글을 썼습니다.

그림 · 스튜디오 청비

기발한 상상력을 바탕으로 새롭고 재미있는 콘텐츠를 만들어 내는 만화 창작 집단입니다. 어린이들이 책을 읽고 큰 꿈을 품기를 바라는 마음으로 즐겁게 작업하고 있습니다. 작품으로 『성철 스님』, 『아 다르고 어 다른 우리말 101가지』, 『반기문 유엔 사무총장의 꿈과 도전』 등이 있습니다.

번역 · 채드 워커(Chad Walker)

미국 텍사스 오스틴에서 심리학과 일본어를 전공했습니다. 일본으로 건너가 10년 간 살았고 이후 한국과 중국을 오가며 한 · 중 · 일의 동아시아 문화를 비교 연구하고 있습니다. 현재는 연세대학교 국어국문학과 박사 과정 중에 있습니다. 옮긴 책으로 『한국어 교육을 위한 한국어 연어사전』, 『한국인의 가치 문화』, 『속성 한국어』 등이 있습니다.

감수 · 김수희

연세대학교에서 역사를 전공했습니다. 이후 한국뿐 아니라 일본, 미국에서 한국어, 일본어, 영어를 가르쳐 왔으며 부모를 위한 영어교육용 책을 썼습니다. 영어교육채널 EBSe '엄마표 영어특강'에서 강의를 하며 홈스쿨, 알파벳과 파닉스, 다차원 테마 영어 수업 기법을 알리고 있습니다. 전국 각지에서 어린이 영어 교육에 대한 강연을 하며 창의적이고 열정적인 교수법으로 영어를 배우고자 하는 어린이와 부모들에게 많은 도움을 주고 있습니다.

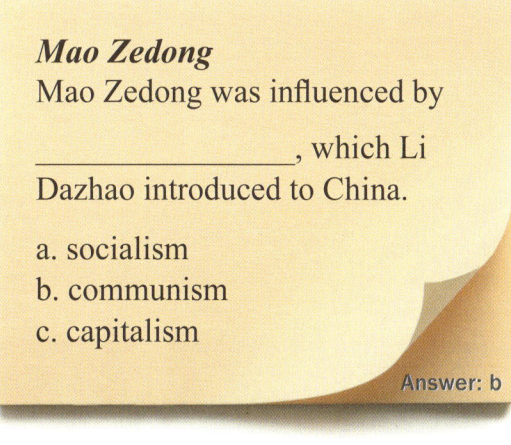

Mao Zedong

Mao Zedong was influenced by
_____, which Li Dazhao introduced to China.

a. socialism
b. communism
c. capitalism

Answer: b

Contents

01   The Rebellious Boy of Shaoshan   10

02   Leaving Home for the Outside World   30

03   Riding the Winds of Revolution   46

04   Awakening to Communism   62

05 Revolution and War 82

06 The Long March for Freedom 104

07 The People's Republic of China 120

Workbook 138

01 The Rebellious Boy of Shaoshan

 Track 01 ▶

Mao Zedong was born in the small village of Shaoshan, located in the city of Xiangtan in Hunan province, China, on December 26, 1893.

Mao's father had grown up poor, but he had worked hard and subsequently became one of the wealthiest men in the village.

Why are you spilling your rice? Eat it all so it's not wasted!

11

To increase the family's wealth, Mao's father made everyone work hard—even little six-year-old Mao.

Son, you can rest if you're tired.

No, if I rest then you'll have to do more work.

In contrast to his father, Mao Zedong's mother had a very kind heart. Mao loved his mother very deeply.

Mother, where did Father go?

He went to another village to take care of some things.

Hmph, he gets to go have fun every day...

Mao's father was extremely angry and beat poor little Mao. Thus, his first confrontation with his father ended in failure.

This won't be the end of it. Next time, I've got to let him know exactly how I feel.

Once he started attending school, Mao Zedong learned how to express himself more boldly. As a result, he found himself having even more arguments with authoritative figures who were self-righteous like his father.

Now that you're in school, you know how to count, right? So now you'll be in charge of our household bookkeeping*.

When I'm not in school I'm busy working in the field, so how do you expect me to have time to do bookkeeping? If you want me to take care of the family's accounts, then you better hire a farmhand to work in the field!

*bookkeeping: The practice of recording the accounts and transactions of a business.

15

Water Margin: One of the four great classical novels of Chinese literature. Written during the Ming Dynasty, it describes the activities of 108 Song Dynasty heroes.
Romance of the Three Kingdoms: One of the four great classical novels of Chinese literature. Written in the 14th century, it describes the actions and events surrounding various heroic characters in China following the fall of the Han Dynasty.

These heroes fought such amazing battles. I wonder if I would ever be able to establish and control an entire country?

Mao Zedong, time to go to school!

Oh! I'll be late again!

Teacher, sorry I'm late!

You've been tardy every day recently! You must be punished!

SLAP

WHACK

17

You worthless little boy.

Well, the stuff you teach is worthless, too! And my guess is that all your students will agree with me on that.

Mao Zedong couldn't stand his teacher, for whom education came second to flaunting his own authority, so one day he ran away from school.

I've had enough. Enough with home, enough with school!

19

I'm hungry... Mother should be cooking rice right about now...

Mother.

After looking everywhere for their lost son for three days, Mao Zedong's family finally found him sleeping in the forest.

Fa-Father...

Get up. Let's go home.

Oh no. He looks really mad.

Once back at home, Mao Zedong waited for his father's scolding. However, his father neither scolded nor beat him. On the contrary, he seemed kinder than before.

For the time being, you can rest here at home. I've already contacted your school, so don't worry about that.

That's strange. I should definitely be in trouble for what I did, so why is he being so nice and not scolding me?

I get it! Rather than my simply following orders obediently, Father only accepts me when I confidently speak my mind.

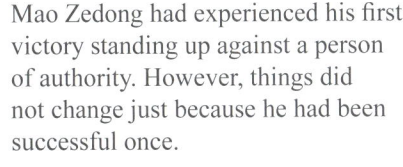

Mao Zedong had experienced his first victory standing up against a person of authority. However, things did not change just because he had been successful once.

According to the Classics*, society's senior members must be compassionate and loving towards others. But Father, not only do you not understand me, but you're always scolding me.

Classics?

Moreover, they also say that seniors should do more work than those younger than they. That's why you should be working much more than me, Father.

*Classics: Books written by or about saints and philosophers.

I send you off to school, and look what you come back with! So now you want to use what you've learned to find fault with your father?

Mao Zedong was no longer a rebellious child. He was now an intelligent young man who could quote from the Classics to criticize his father's behavior and justify his own position.

Son, you can't do that. Apologize to your father.

No! I have no need for an apology from such an irreverent boy.

Hmph, there's no sense in arguing with him if he's gonna use those books to find fault with me.

If that's the way it's going to be, then I'll have to change tactics. Humiliating him in public should teach him not to mess with me.

Stop!

What are
you doing?

Please
apologize!

28

From this experience, Mao Zedong learned that the courage to face danger was necessary to achieve his goals. Standing up to his father in this way taught Mao how to confront those with a lot of power.

Leaving Home for the Outside World

02

🎧 CD1 **Track 11** ▶

Now a young man, Mao Zedong studied the Classics and writing under a young law student and an elderly scholar named Mao Luzhong. This was also the first time Mao Zedong had left his hometown village and heard stories about the outside world.

Oh my! The state of the nation is getting serious. It seems the entire world will soon erupt in chaos.

What do you mean?

The emperor's daily banquets are bankrupting the country, and to make up for it they're raising taxes on the common people.

All the common people won't like this. Voices of discontent can already be heard all over the country.

What? Are you saying that's happening to our country right now?

It's no wonder you haven't heard about it. I imagine such news doesn't reach remote areas like Shaoshan.

Mao Zedong, don't you think you'll feel a bit stifled living your whole life in your small village? City life, on the other hand...

Mao Zedong broadened his view of the world by reading the newspapers and magazines he had access to while studying.

Wow, I had no idea the world was going through so much change. I too want to go to the city.

31

Yep, it's time for me to leave this place.

Mao Zedong wanted to go to the city and attend a modern school, because there he could learn about Western science, sports, music, world history, and foreign languages, among other things.

Why can't I go? Even if you don't permit me to go, I plan to leave this place!

Everyone who lives here is oblivious to what's happening in the world. It's a life of ignorance.

If I say no, that means no!

But why? I just want to learn more about the world!

Haven't you learned enough already? Why does a farmer need to know science and history? Do you know how much money I've already spent on you to study?

Money! Money! Money! Please stop talking about money!

You ungrateful boy!

However, Mao Zedong's fascination with the outside world did not lessen.

I won't change my mind no matter how much you object, Father.

You pathetic boy! Far be it for you to want to help out your family as soon as possible by making some money.

33

 **Track 13** ▶

Determined to change his mind, starting the next day Mao Zedong began following his father around relentlessly.

It doesn't matter how many times you tell me, I'm not going to change my mind.

Father, with a modern education I can get a job that pays even more money.

Hmm, I guess you have a point.

Yay! So you'll give me permission?

Upon receiving his father's permission, Mao Zedong promptly prepared for his departure. Then, in 1910, he enrolled in a modern school in the town of Xiangxiang, where his mother's family lived.

Xiangxiang was a world full of new and marvelous things. Having spent all of his life in a village separated from the outside world, Xiangxiang was a place where Mao Zedong could meet and talk with people from many different places.

Wow, the city is even more extraordinary than I had imagined!

Did you see the military parade yesterday? Wasn't it really impressive?

Yes, it was. I want to become a soldier.

Hey, are you going to the commemorative celebration for Xi Taihou*?

Of course!

Hey guys, who's Xi Taihou?

What? You don't know Xi Taihou, the woman who controlled the Qing Dynasty* for 50 years? Have you been living under a rock?

Um...

A real live caveman.

*Xi Taihou: Famous Chinese female leader who ruled the Qing Dynasty with great power and authority.
*Qing Dynasty: The final Chinese dynasty, lasting from 1616 to 1912.

*Peter the Great: Emperor of Russia who expanded and strengthened his country.
*Napoleon: Emperor of France who conquered Europe.

What did you say? I guess you have no idea just how great Napoleon was!

Mao Zedong, those are just imaginary people who only exist in novels.

Historical novels aren't just made-up stories!

Novels are nothing more than novels. They're all just creations of the author.

So are you saying that Confucius and Mencius are also imaginary? I learned about them through historical novels, too.

No, they're different.

And just how are they different?

Mao Zedong's anger didn't end there. He started gathering signatures from the other students to get the teacher expelled from school.

So what exactly did our teacher do wrong?

What? Are you a fool? You don't even realize you're being treated unfairly...

Principal, how can a person who doesn't know the difference between fact and fiction teach history?

You shrewd little boy. Do you actually think you can get your history teacher replaced?

Yes. We have a right to receive a proper, correct education.

You can't expect to get a person fired just because they think differently from you. That's enough. Go now.

I see you're no different than our history teacher! How did such an ignorant person become the school principal?

40

Mao Zedong had failed in his attempt to get the history teacher replaced. The cost of his behavior was expulsion from school, less than one year after he had enrolled.

What Mao Zedong would experience next would change his life forever.

*uprising: A popular rebellion against a government or its policies.

The man was referring to the uprising of starving peasants who had captured the flags of the ruling Qing Dynasty and taken over the local government offices.

In an effort to defuse the anger among the peasant farmers, the Qing government announced it would distribute grain to all farmers who gathered in a certain location. This, however, was a trick. The government quickly arrested and killed everyone who showed up.

Learning about this incident caused Mao Zedong to feel anger and hostility toward his country.

I can't believe they promised to give the farmers food, and then killed them all!

The government tricked the peasants by making a false promise. Something must be done about this.

Without any definite plans, Mao Zedong set off for Changsha, the capital of Hunan Province, in the hope of fighting alongside the peasant farmers. Changsha was a much bigger and more modern city that Xiangxiang.

03 . Riding the Winds of Revolution

CD1 Track 19 ▶

In 1911, Mao Zedong enrolled in a new school in Changsha. Here, he had access to even more news and information regarding current events.

There's a revolution being planned. Before long, China too will be reformed.

Revolution?

They say they're going to oust the corrupted government and emperor and build a new country.

Revolution, reform...

After witnessing the country's tyranny during the peasant uprising, Mao Zedong was deeply moved by this talk of a revolution.

Just like the other students, Mao Zedong also wished for change for his country. After witnessing authoritative and violent figures since he was a young boy, he now wanted to be at the forefront of the revolution to throw out the outdated, traditional ways of doing things.

Is this really going to happen?

It most certainly is. The situation is already quite serious.

But a revolution is easier said than done. Just like last time...

This time is different. Thousands have already come together to form a plan.

The Qing Dynasty was facing crises both inside and outside its borders. From within, the hearts of the people were in disarray from the abuses of governmental corruption, while from the outside the powerful European nations were threatening the throne by launching invasions.

47

It was true. The rebels had started a revolution to topple a feudal dynasty that risked the country with its poor decision.

Out with this corrupt dynasty!

Fight!

BOOM

BANG BANG

It was October 10, 1911. The revolution had been ignited by mutiny in the eastern city of Wuchang, in Hubei province, and spread all across the country in less than a month.

Yaaaah!

Mao Zedong began reading a newspaper called *Minbo*, or *The People's Report*, published by the resistance group, the Chinese Revolutionary Alliance which would later grow into a political party called the Chinese Nationalist Party. The Party's founding goals included "the expulsion of the Manchus, and the recovery of China."

The paper supported Sun Yat-sen as leader of the revolution, and it urged readers to cut off their traditional pigtals* as a sign of protest against the corrupt Qing government.

I will cut my pigtail off.

Mao Zedong immediately cut off his pigtail, and then tried to convince his classmates to do the same.

Do you all think the revolution under way is justified?

Of course we do.

*pigtail: A long braid of hair worn hanging down the back of the neck, with the sides and top of the head shaven off.

50

The revolutionaries are out there risking their lives fighting, and you can't even cut off some of your hair? If you really support the cause, how can you just stand there doing nothing?

Good. Who's next?

I'll do it.

Me, too.

And me!

Deeply impressed by the ideas of Sun Yat-sen, Mao Zedong posted a manifesto on the school wall describing those ideas in his own words.

We've got to do whatever we can to help the revolution, no matter how small.

Hmm? What's that?

What a piece of writing! It could convince even the most ardent skeptic.

Mao Zedong took note of how his manifesto influenced those who read it on the wall. Later in life he would continue to use it to get his meaning across to others.

That November, a military uprising led by the revolutionary army occurred in Wuhan, a city about 250 miles from Changsha. Upon learning of the uprising, Mao Zedong and his friends decided to join the revolutionary army there.

However, the army had already successfully advanced into Changsha before they had even left.

Wow, the revolutionary army is here!

Look at how quick and skillful the army leaders are. Isn't it amazing?

To think they could make it all the way here while we were still preparing to leave! Let's go and join them.

Alright, let's do it.

However, before long internal divisions arose which discouraged the revolutionary army's popular supporters.

Unhappy with the course the revolution was taking, a number of army leaders joined forces with corrupt government officials and killed a number of important revolutionary leaders.

This wasn't the kind of revolution we had in mind!

It can't be!

In this way, we can't succeed in reforming. We need a systematic organization so we can work in harmony.

I can't understand why members of the same revolutionary army would turn their guns on themselves when they're supposed to be toppling a corrupt government! Does power make everyone change?

The sight before him made Mao Zedong wonder if an even stronger leader might be necessary to lead the people in their revolution.

I should enter the military and learn the art of consolidating power.

After careful consideration, Mao Zedong made the decision to join the government's own regular army.

Mao Zedong's life as a soldier was peaceful. Using his military salary, he bought books, magazines, and newspapers to read. It was at this time that Mao first learned about socialism.

A classless society in which everyone does the same amount of work and wealth is distributed equally... Interesting indeed.

Around this time, the revolutionary forces had emerged victorious in their long battle to oust the corrupt Qing Dynasty. In February of 1912, the last emperor of China, Puyi, was forced to abdicate the throne, ending 300 years of Qing imperial rule over China.

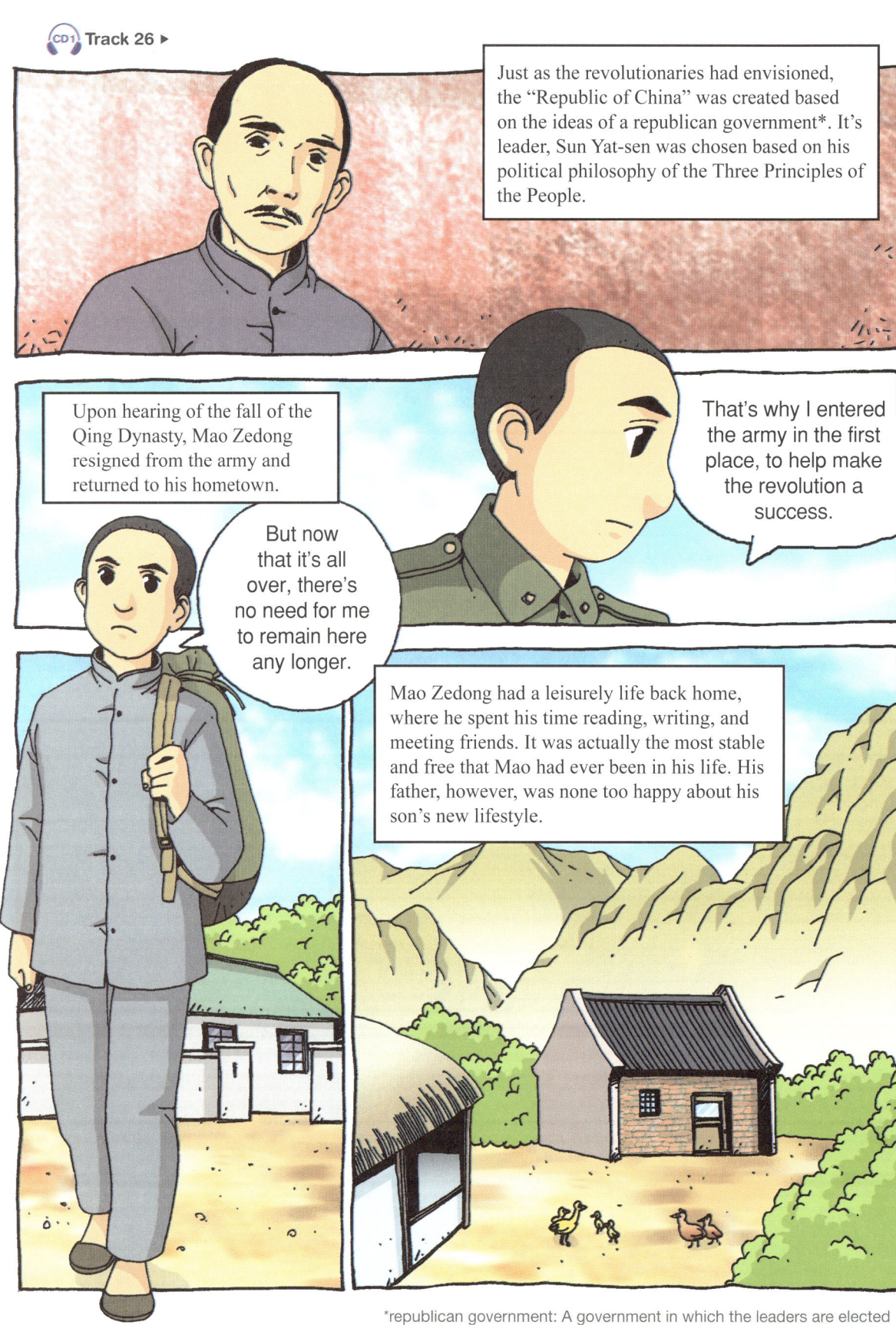

Just as the revolutionaries had envisioned, the "Republic of China" was created based on the ideas of a republican government*. It's leader, Sun Yat-sen was chosen based on his political philosophy of the Three Principles of the People.

Upon hearing of the fall of the Qing Dynasty, Mao Zedong resigned from the army and returned to his hometown.

That's why I entered the army in the first place, to help make the revolution a success.

But now that it's all over, there's no need for me to remain here any longer.

Mao Zedong had a leisurely life back home, where he spent his time reading, writing, and meeting friends. It was actually the most stable and free that Mao had ever been in his life. His father, however, was none too happy about his son's new lifestyle.

*republican government: A government in which the leaders are elected and granted the authority to govern by the people.

I think you've played around enough. Now that you're an adult, it's time you got a job and started earning your keep!

Father, you're exactly right. That's why I plan to become a teacher.

Mao Zedong decided to become a teacher so that he could instill in children the right-minded thinking he had been reading about. In 1913, Mao enrolled in the First Provincial Normal School of Hunan province.

04 Awakening to Communism

 Track 27 ▶

Mao Zedong studied hard, and earned his teaching qualification five years later. Even then, however, the political scene in China was still unstable.

Hmm, I expected the situation to have changed by the time I finished school... But it looks like nothing has changed at all.

What can I do with just a teaching certificate? No schools are hiring.

A lot of my friends are now preparing to go abroad.

At the time, the Western world was in the middle of World War I, the effects of which reached as far as Asia. China was still in a state of upheaval. The chosen leader of the new Republic of China, Sun Yat-sen, had been driven out of power in a matter of days by Yuan Shikai*, a politician funded by wealthy landowners and foreign money.

What's happening to our country? Just look at all the starving people.

Our leaders are all busy filling their own pockets. I don't see any difference between them and the old Qing Dynasty.

Let's rise and fight again, like we did before. I ask you, would you rather die starving, or fighting?

Right.

He's right!

Let's do it!

*Yuan Shikai: A Chinese politician who subjugated the provisional government of the Republic of China and seized control while setting up a military government.

They're right. We've got to start fighting back. But this town is too small to work from. We should move to a larger city, from which we can draw up bigger plans.

With the help of one of his college professors, Mao Zedong got a job at the library at Beijing University. He promptly left his hometown of Hunan province for Beijing, the largest city in China.

Wow, Beijing is really big. I hope I can make it here.

Hey, Mao Zedong! Long time no see. I see you made it here okay.

Yes, and I owe it all to you for giving me this opportunity.

Well, I'm confident you'll be able to learn much more while you are here.

Mao Zedong read all the important books he could find while working at the library. He also continued to study in his free time and attended political discussion groups.

Sorry I'm late again.

No problem. Did you just get off work today, too?

Yes.

You're a hard worker. There aren't many young people like you these days. Very admirable, indeed.

It was a time when a number of communists had come together in Beijing. Mao Zedong began learning about communism and its possible plans for the future of China.

Hi. I'm Chen Duxiu.

I'm Li Dazhao.

Chen Duxiu started the magazine *New Youth*, which was very influential in ousting the Qing Dynasty from power.

Nice to meet you.

Li Dazhao is the founder of a Marxism* study group. He's trying to introduce his ideas to China.

It's a pleasure to meet you, Mr. Li Dazhao.

As the person who introduced communism to China, Li Dazhao had a very big influence on Mao Zedong.

*Marxism: A school of thought that believes a working class revolution is necessary to correct the wrongs of capitalist societies.

69

Through his talks with Li Dazhao, Mao Zedong gained a much better understanding of the ideas of communism.

This is it! Communism is exactly what China needs to get out of its current state of chaos.

Mao Zedong!

Your mother has suffered a fall.

70

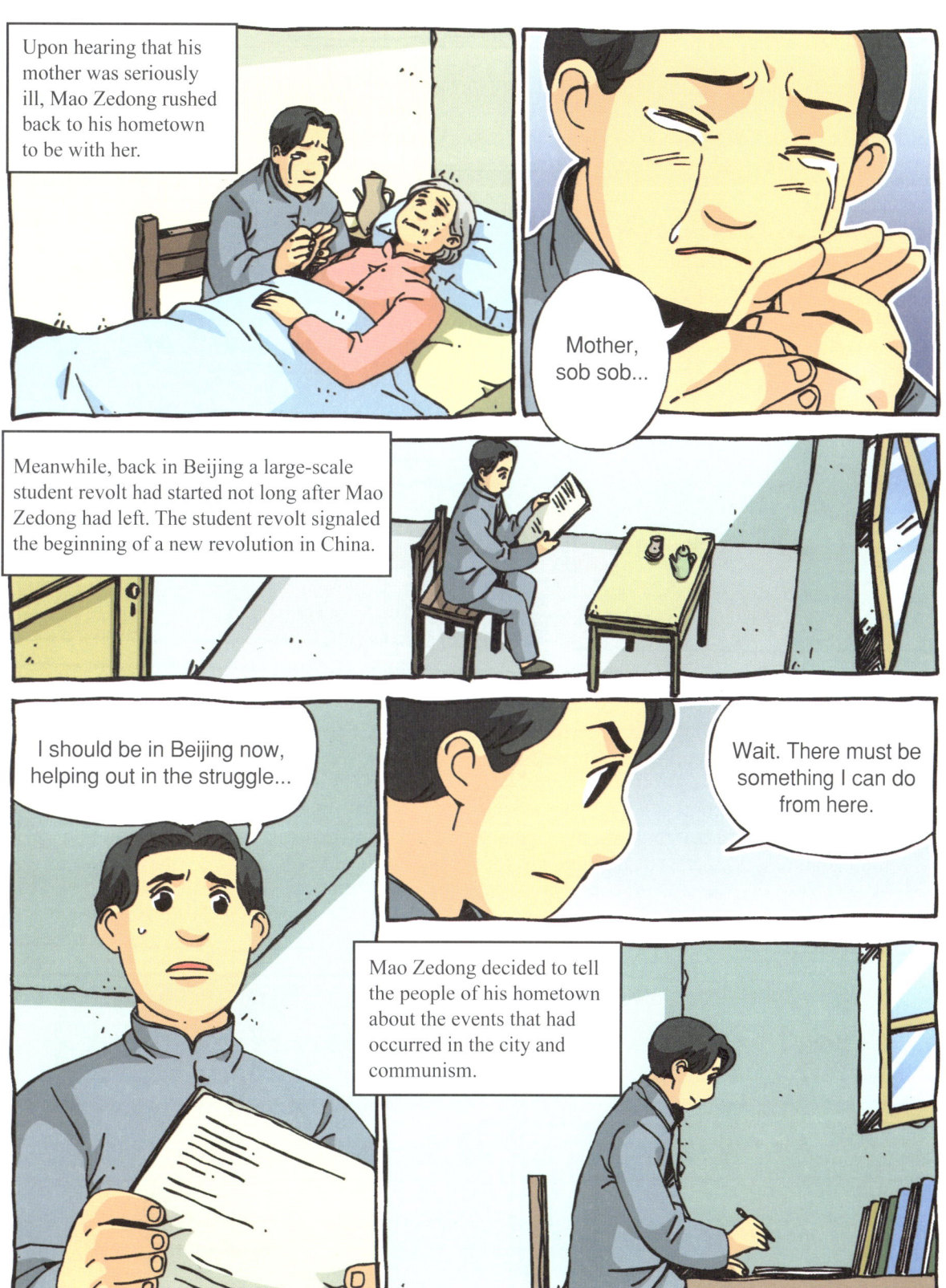

Upon hearing that his mother was seriously ill, Mao Zedong rushed back to his hometown to be with her.

Mother, sob sob...

Meanwhile, back in Beijing a large-scale student revolt had started not long after Mao Zedong had left. The student revolt signaled the beginning of a new revolution in China.

I should be in Beijing now, helping out in the struggle...

Wait. There must be something I can do from here.

Mao Zedong decided to tell the people of his hometown about the events that had occurred in the city and communism.

There are student demonstrations currently under way in Beijing. To make sure the student movement doesn't stop there, it is our duty to make this into a political struggle.

Mao Zedong started the weekly journal *Xiangjiang Review*, which he wrote, published, and distributed himself.

How China Should Be United

China is currently being governed according to the same bad policies used by the old Qing Dynasty. However, progress cannot be made by blindly following the past. We must therefore actively question and correct those things that are wrong in all aspects of our lives, including religion, politics, society, education, and the economy. Let us make ourselves be heard through strikes and peaceful demonstrations!

True indeed! Every word of this is right.

Mao Zedong is right. We can't leave things as they are. We all should join him.

The *Xiangjiang Review* was very well received. The first 2,000 copies of the first issue sold out in a single day, and by the time the fourth issue was published, readership had grown to over 5,000.

How dare he call for a revolution!

Get this journal to cease publication immediately!

Mao Zedong's editorial office, full of his supporters, was normally a place of bustling activity. However, everyone stopped in their tracks the instant soldiers sent by the local warlord*, Zhang Jingyao, arrived on the scene.

Me. Is there a problem?

Which of you is Mao Zedong?

This journal is to cease publication after today! All materials here will be confiscated.

Now get moving, fast!

Yes, sir!

*warlord: Independent military factions, or cliques, managed and operated by powerful local government officials.

What is this!
Please stop
this instant!

We've got to work
together and stop
them from doing
this!

Do they really
think this will stop
me? There are lots
of magazines
I can write for.
Just wait and
see!

Zhang Jingyao sent soldiers to the school and brought the students under control. Mao Zedong was branded as a dangerous individual for instigating the student demonstrations.

Wh-what's the matter?

Mao, your mother has passed away.

What? No, that can't be true!

Mother!

Unlike his strict father, Mao Zedong's mother had always been tender and kind toward everyone. She had taught Mao how to really love someone.

Mother... You showed me how to love, and now it's time for me to put it into practice.

Now that his mother had passed away, there was no longer any reason for Mao Zedong to stay in Changsha. He returned to Beijing, where more sad news was waiting for him. His mentor, who had taught him how to survive the Beijing city life, had also passed away.

To think that I would also lose my greatest mentor... How am I to go on?

But the fight against Zhang Jingyao is not over. I can't give up now.

With renewed determination, Mao Zedong sought out Chen Duxiu to ask for help with the demonstrations he had started back home.

So, what did you come to see me about?

Professor, I'm leading a fight against the military warlord and his clique in Changsha. But they are just too powerful compared to us.

Hmm.

At that time, Chen Duxiu had been getting communists together to form a new communist political party, and therefore had goals very similar to those of Mao Zedong. He was delighted to help Mao.

Okay. If there's anything I can do to help, just let me know.

Thank you, Professor!

05 •Revolution and War

 Track 01 ▶

In the summer of 1921, Mao Zedong and other communists gathered in Shanghai to hold the first session of the National Congress of the Communist Party of China.

We're finally taking the first step toward clearing up the chaotic state of the country.

At the time, the Chinese Communist Party had only about 50 members. Many people still did not know much about communism, and Mao Zedong was simply considered one of the new young communist scholars.

First Session of the National Congress of the Communist Party of China

I hereby begin the first session of the...

Disband at once!

This is an illegal gathering. If you are ever caught doing this again, I won't be so nice!

Comrades.

We've come this far, so I see no reason to give up at this point.

Right. However, now that they know of our existence, they'll constantly be after us. I think we should lay low for a while.

In that case, let's separate for a few days and then meet up again.

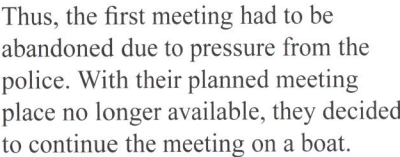
Thus, the first meeting had to be abandoned due to pressure from the police. With their planned meeting place no longer available, they decided to continue the meeting on a boat.

We need to increase our membership. Let's each go to different parts of the country, and get together all the laborers who want to join us.

Mao Zedong and the other young party members each went to their assigned locations and educated the masses. In this way, the communists gained influence and power.

If we're going to succeed, we must first expel the warlords.

Whew, the more the warlords oppress us, the harder it is for us to stay active.

But we're still too weak to do that.

In 1923, having joined forces with the Nationalist Party, the Chinese Communist Party began operating as a full-fledged organization. Mao Zedong was very active in both groups.

However, the leader of the Nationalists, Sun Yat-sen, fell ill, and soon a rift emerged between the Communists and the Nationalists. This rift was caused by Nationalist member Chiang Kai-shek, who had a disposition entirely different from Sun Yat-sen and was becoming more and more powerful.

Chiang Kai-shek is getting more powerful day by day.

There's no need to worry. He won't do anything to break up our alliance.

This is not the time for such optimism. What I mean is Chiang Kai-shek used Sun Yat-sen's illness as an excuse to become leader of their party!

The other party members don't act on something until it becomes urgent. And once that happens, it will be too late...

Just as Mao Zedong had expected, Chiang Kai-shek began consolidating his power by partnering with the faction warlords.

This guy is taking control of the military, too! At this rate Chiang Kai-shek will make himself king!

Well, there's no sense worrying about this all by myself. Nobody else will listen to me.

88

Mao Zedong was tired of being around people who took such a casual attitude in the face of imminent crisis. He resolved to forget everything and return to his hometown.

Hum, I guess there's nothing more that I can do here!

Around that time, Sun Yat-sen passed away. In his will, he had written "The Revolution is not yet accomplished!"

Oh no, not Sun Yat-sen!

I didn't think this day would come so soon... Sun Yat-sen, you were the father of China's revolution.

I won't forget what you fought for.

What will happen to the Communist Party now?

Back home in Shaoshan, Mao Zedong opened a night school to teach writing and communism to Hunan province peasant farmers.

Is each of you currently getting justly compensated for the amount of work you do?

I work day in and day out, with no rest, but I've never eaten my fill at the dinner table.

Me, either.

But the landowners don't do any work, and yet they live like kings just because they own land.

As Mao Zedong observed that the Hunan province farmers had a stronger desire to learn than anyone else he had ever taught, he naturally developed an even greater interest in their plight.

Then, one day Mao Zedong discovered that the farmers had hidden potential.

What could they be doing?

It's hard enough getting by on just one meal a day, and now the taxes are going up again.

Some of us work our fingers to the bone, while others just squander their money away. The world is really unfair.

They must think we are pushovers because we never speak up.

You're right. We shouldn't just stand around doing nothing.

Hmm, the tyranny of the landowners continues unabated.

Mao Zedong now took a renewed interest in farmers. They comprised the majority of China's population, and Mao realized that their combined strength would be more powerful than that of any other social class.

It's time to unite the farmers!

Mao Zedong formed a peasant union* to give the peasants a way to collectively voice their dissatisfaction. Soon similar peasant unions had sprung up all across Hunan province to stand up against the power of the landlords.

*union: A group of people who join together to realize their shared goals.

The peasants' actions angered the landowners, who had until then reaped all the rewards of the peasants' constant sacrifices.

Where did that guy Mao come from?

Mao Zedong is inciting the peasants to fight. We can't afford to let the situation escalate further.

The Hunan province military warlords, worried about the peasant resistance activities, decided to capture and arrest Mao Zedong.

I can't see Mao Zedong.

Look in every nook and cranny! Even if he escaped, he couldn't have gone far!

If I get arrested now, all of our efforts will have been for nothing. I can't let myself get caught.

After a successful escape, Mao Zedong started working to spread the peasant resistance into a full-scale movement. However, now another obstacle was waiting for him.

General Chiang Kai-shek, everyone is here now.

Really? Can you see Mao Zedong?

Yes, he's in the middle of giving a speech.

The landowners' moncy and military are necessary for our plans. That's why troublemakers like Mao Zedong must be eliminated.

Yes, I understand, sir.

Just as Mao Zedong had predicted, Chiang Kai-shek severed ties with the Communist Party as soon as he took over as leader of the Nationalist Party. He then branded all the chief Communist Party members, including Mao, as traitors and persecuted them.

Ladies and gentlemen, who have we worked for so hard for all these years?

BANG

BANG

Aaah! Help!

We demand just compensation for our work!

Ahh!

Wh-what is happening?

The Nationalists' attacks dealt a severe blow to the peasant unions. Once numbering in the millions, their membership was now a mere few thousand, and their confidence had been crushed. Pulling himself together, Mao Zedong gathered the remaining peasants and returned to his hometown.

On September 9, 1927, the peasant union members fought a battle with Nationalists who had followed them into the mountains.

The peasant farmers were no match for the well-trained Nationalist army. Mao Zedong had once again suffered a disastrous defeat.

Do you know how many casualties we suffered?

There are now less than a thousand of us remaining. Moreover, a lot of them are talking about quitting the fight.

I see...

Despite our tireless efforts, this is how we ended up.

No, Commander. The fight's not over yet.

I feel deeply ashamed for making those peasant farmers face a trained army. I was too short-sighted.

I beg your pardon? Commander, you can't quit now.

Quit? Of course not! I'm simply saying I regret putting everyone through all this.

Don't worry about us. We're here to fight for a life where everyone can live well, just like you said, Commander.

Alright, then, we shall carry on the fight. Actually, tomorrow I've arranged for the other Communist Party leaders to meet here. It will be our new beginning.

Yes, sir, Commander!

Yes, it's all going to turn out just fine.

103

06 The Long March for Freedom

Mao Zedong met with the other Communist Party leaders and moved to the Jinggang Mountains, in eastern Hunan province. The rugged mountainous terrain was just the right cover they needed to develop their new plan in secret.

Make sure you're hidden well, and then try to find their center of operations. Then we'll quickly launch our military strike and disappear.

Yes, sir!

104

107

You can rest in peace here. Your death will not be in vain. We will succeed.

By the time Mao Zedong arrived in the Jinggang Mountains, his army numbered less than a thousand. This displeased the Communist Party leadership, who proceeded to take disciplinary measures against him.

A lot of communist party members have died because of your decisions.

The circumstances were unavoidable.

You're not qualified to be a leader. You should have been more concerned about protecting your men than waging battles.

If we hadn't fought back we all would have died. We had no other choice but to fight!

A likely excuse. Right now, there are even people in the Communist Party claiming that you are hindering the revolutionary cause!

Okay, so how do you explain the loss of so many of our party comrades under your leadership?

I did my best. But aren't some sacrifices necessary if we are to achieve our larger goals?

Hmph, so why were you practically the only one who escaped such sacrifices?

How dare you make such an insulting remark!

At its last meeting, the Communist Party decided to strip you of all your party leadership authority, effective immediately.

It can't be!

You should consider yourself lucky. Death would have been a better punishment considering the things you did...

Despite being the most ardent supporter of the Communist Party since its inception, Mao Zedong had been stripped of all authority and degraded to common party member status.

Haha. Hahaha!

111

I need this rice to have energy to keep going. We have to keep going for everyone's sake, including your brother and the other innocent farmers who lost their lives along the way! That's the only way we will live to fight again!

Although he had lost all official authority given to him by the Communist Party, Mao Zedong had not lost sight of his dream. The sound of his heartfelt cry reverberated throughout the soldiers' hearts.

I've never considered giving up. That would be betraying all of you! I'm not afraid to die. The only thing I'm afraid of is disappointing all of you who believe in me!

I will never break my promise to you! We will succeed in creating a society in which everyone has a good life!

112

Until then, I can't let myself die even if I want to.

Sob, sob... Commander... I'm so sorry.

Mao Zedong and his followers marched more than 6,000 miles. They crossed rivers and mountains, and passed through deserts and swamps where all sorts of dangers lurked.

The Nationalists continued to pursue them. While a few other Communist Party commanders tried to help out Mao, in the end they couldn't keep up with him. Thus Mao and his soldiers were left with nobody but themselves to rely on.

Don't worry, Commander. We all believe in you.

You really believe in someone who's been abandoned by even his own party?

Yes. Because no matter what anyone else says, you are the one who never gave up on us, or on the revolution.

Right. My guess is that the Communist Party is regretting their decision to let you go.

Hahaha, I appreciate that.

Don't lose courage. We will stay by your side no matter what, Commander.

Successfully evading capture by the Nationalists, Mao Zedong's march to acquire more and more comrades for the revolutionary cause continued. However, their situation only worsened with time. Soon Mao and his soldiers had to survive on only fruit and grass for sustenance.

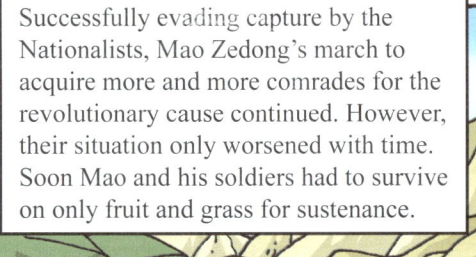

The soldiers had to endure nights of freezing cold and days of uncomfortable humidity. Many soldiers died from malnutrition and food poisoning. However, as the days went on attacks from the Nationalists decreased.

In October 1935, Mao Zedong and 8,000 soldiers arrived in the western China province of Shaanxi, where other Communist Party military units were waiting.

We're in trouble. It seems the Nationalists have discovered our location.

They sure are relentless. We never get a moment's rest.

We have no time to lose. We must leave as soon as the injured soldiers have been treated.

Okay. The soldiers have had a chance to eat and get some rest, so we'll prepare to leave at first light tomorrow morning.

With renewed energy Mao Zedong and the newly reunited Communists fought side-by-side against the Nationalists.

Fear not! We will be victorious!

Fight!

07 The People's Republic of China

 Track 20 ▶

Emerging victorious in the fight against the Nationalists, Mao Zedong returned to the Communist Party with dignity.

Now all those commanders who ran from the fight to save their own skins are trying to return.

But what kind of revolution can those who abandoned their comrades ever hope to realize?

Mao Zedong proceeded to purge the party of all the commanders who had caused problems by forsaking their soldiers in battle and not supporting the party's objectives.

We've been through so much to get to this point. Those who have more than others, and those who betray the party for the sake of their own lives will not be forgiven!

Mao Zedong later would stand tall as leader of the Communist Party. From the party base in Yan'an, a city in northern Shaanxi province, Mao developed his new policies for government.

The U.S. is offering to help the Communists and Nationalists reconcile their differences.

That's good news. We've spent so much energy fighting the Nationalists, so wouldn't anything that could better our relationship with them be of great benefit?

Comrade, do you really believe the Nationalists? They don't even hesitate to use their guns on civilians.

But after all this fighting, they too must have realized that something must be done to change the situation.

For the time being, let's just wait and see what happens.

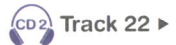 **Track 22** ▶

However, while the Communists and Nationalists were fighting within China's borders, Japan invaded China from the outside, igniting the Second Sino-Japanese War.

Major news! Japan has attacked China!

I can't believe war has broken out in this difficult time...

First and foremost, we have to protect the country from Japan. We'll need to join forces with the Nationalists.

Mao Zedong made the offer to join forces with the Nationalists to fight Japan. Chiang Kai-shek agreed to Mao's proposal, and they entered the war together.

This goes against my better judgment, but we have no other choice.

However, as soon as the war ended with Japan's surrender on August 15, 1945, the Communist and Nationalist forces resumed fighting over who would control the land that Japan had occupied during the war.

Oh dear, war is starting once again.

Chiang Kai-shek is still treating the Communists with contempt.

In 1948, the Communists launched a full-scale revolution, and successfully removed the Nationalists from power.

Victory is near!

Yay!

Fight to the end!

The Communists took over Shanghai, China's largest city, and then eventually captured Chengdu, which was the last Nationalist-occupied city in mainland China. With nowhere else to go, Chiang Kai-shek and the Nationalist Party fled to the island of Taiwan*.

*Taiwan: A big island off the southeast coast of China. Chiang Kai-shek set up a new government there and became its president.

After finally seizing victory in the fight with the Nationalists, on October 1, 1949, Mao Zedong declared the establishment of the People's Republic of China, and became its chairman*.

*chairman: The highest office (or person) in a government or political party.

Chairman Mao Zedong's first order of business was to increase the number of available jobs. To give farmers new job opportunities, he created businesses that relied on human labor rather than machines.

Finally we're going to be compensated fairly for the amount of work we do.

I've been a farmer my whole life. Will I be able to do one of these new jobs?

I don't care how difficult it is, it will surely be better than working under a corrupt warlord.

However, Mao's reforms didn't happen as he had envisioned. Failed attempts at industrialization and wrong-headed policies resulted in even more people starving and dying than ever before.

Feelings of betrayal started growing among the people. Dissenters even emerged within the Communist Party itself, throwing Chinese society once again into chaos.

131

Mao Zedong took a cold-hearted stance towards those who opposed him, purging everyone who disagreed with his policies.

I have no need for anyone who doesn't follow the party line. Throw them all into prison!

Those who witnessed such actions by the government grew fearful of Mao's authority. They started blindly obeying Mao Zedong, as if he were a god.

In the end, Mao Zedong's social reforms failed to create the egalitarian, utopian society he had dreamed of. China had become an even more autocratic society than it had been under the Nationalists.

Th-this is wrong. These are not the reforms... I had in mind.

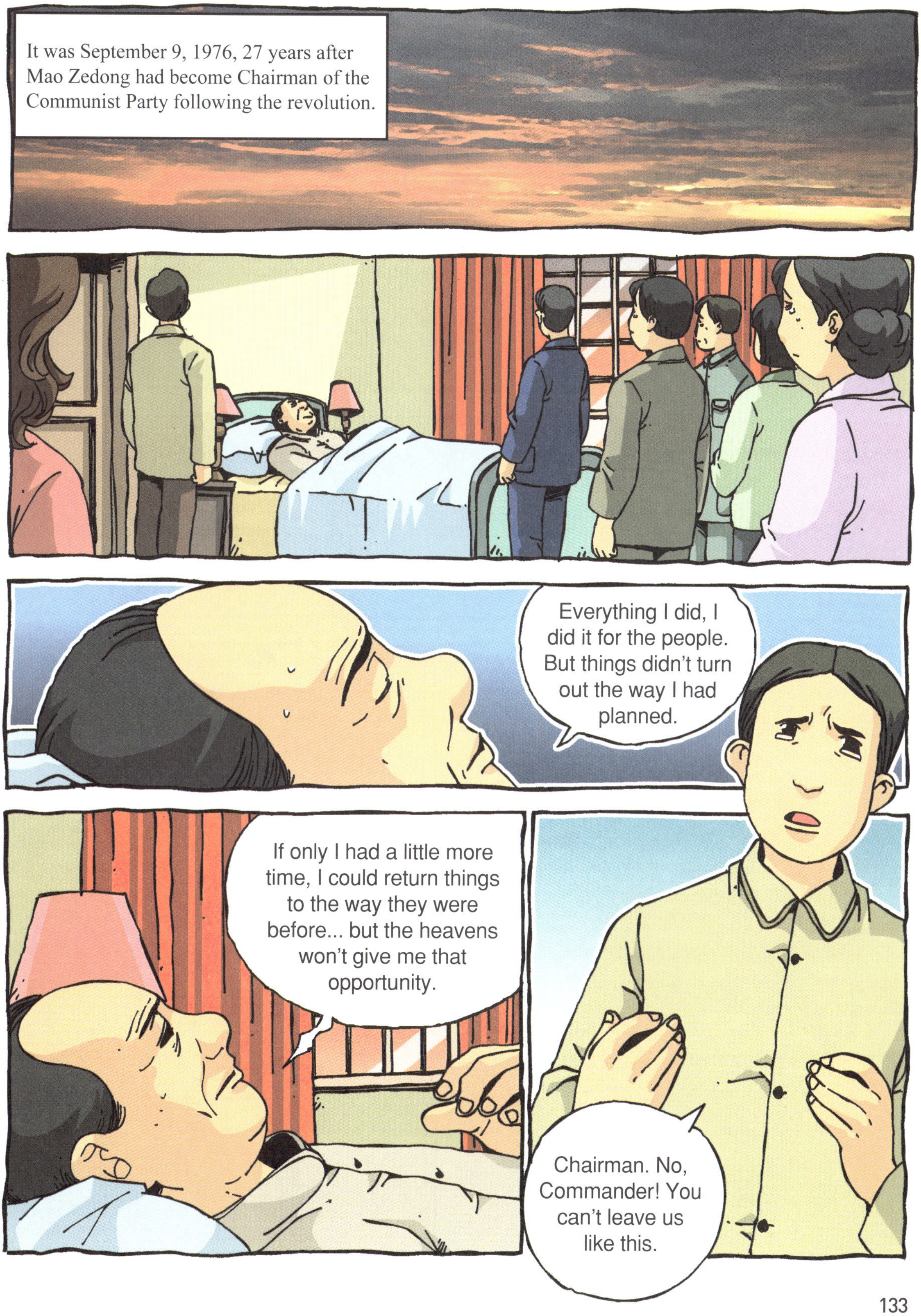

It was September 9, 1976, 27 years after Mao Zedong had become Chairman of the Communist Party following the revolution.

Everything I did, I did it for the people. But things didn't turn out the way I had planned.

If only I had a little more time, I could return things to the way they were before... but the heavens won't give me that opportunity.

Chairman. No, Commander! You can't leave us like this.

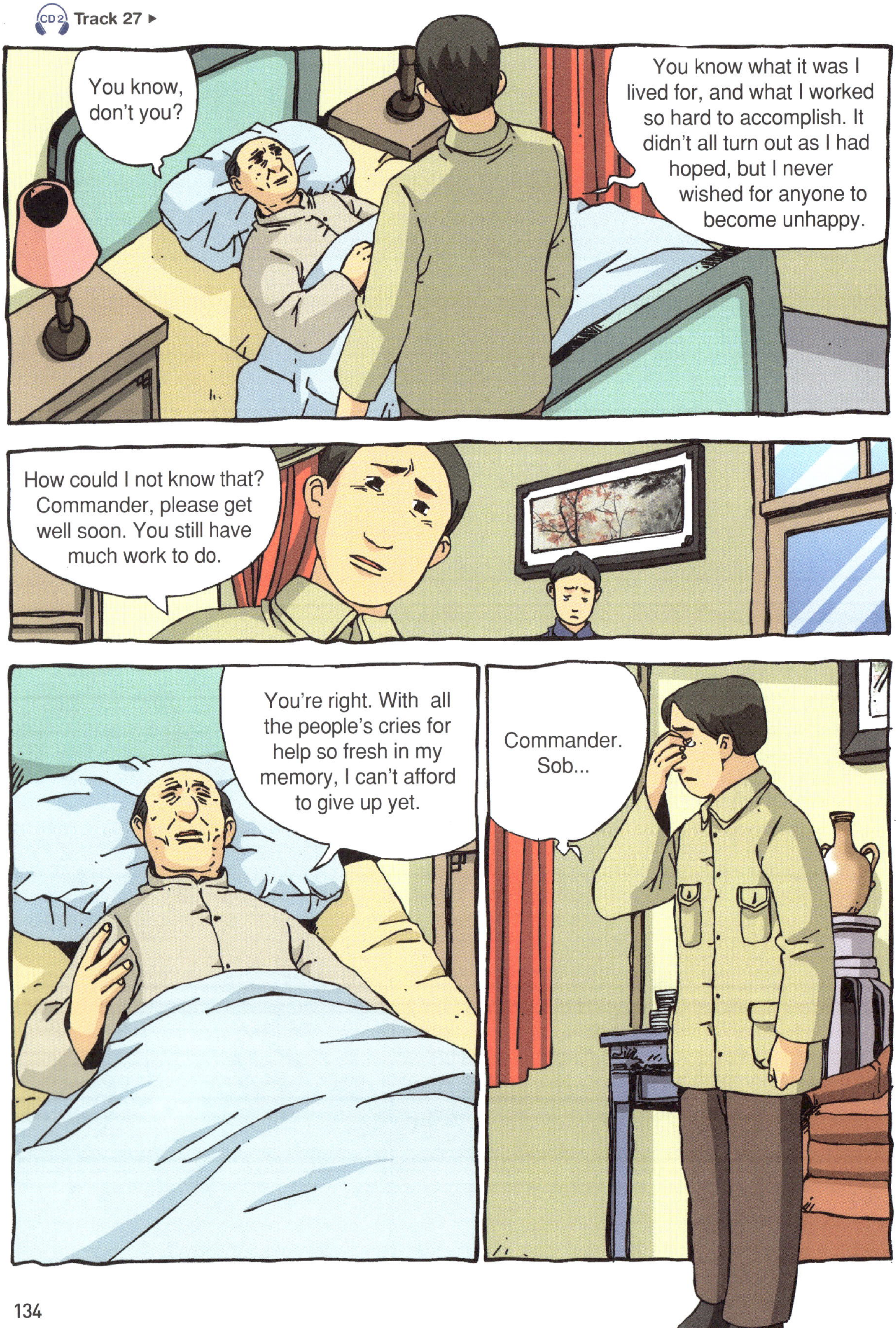

Revolution is not a dinner party, nor an essay, nor a painting, nor a piece of embroidery; it cannot be advanced softly, gradually, carefully, considerably, respectfully, politely, plainly, and modestly. A revolution is an unavoidable process we must go through in order to create a better society.

Many people consider China to be the world's second largest superpower, after the United States. Mao Zedong was the person who wholeheartedly ushered China into the modern world, despite numerous setbacks along the way. Thus, you cannot fully understand China's present and future without first understanding Mao Zedong.

Born the son of a farmer, Mao Zedong grew up to be the leader of the most populous country on earth. Subsequent generations have both criticized him as a dictator and praised him as a powerful leader. However, nobody disputes his prominent place in Chinese history.

Mao Zedong began what would continue as a strong, centralized government in China, and the principles of communism for which he staked his entire life still form China's basic governing ideology. This is precisely why Mao Zedong is still an extremely important person to over 1.3 billion Chinese people today.

Word Search

● Find the words which are hidden horizontally, vertically and diagonally.

```
S M Z G Q M Z G Q M Z G Q Q M Z G Q M X
W O I N A E N T I E S T A B L I S H N O
E B M J W B Q J E T E A R B A R I O B M
R V C P A D C K R V V K P R V C K M V M
O C T O K S E N T C A L T R C D U K C E
B X E Q E N E O Y X I Q Y O E N O X M
L Z V W N D I W C Z R W R U Z P J N Z W
I N A E I A E O I A R Z E I A R E E A I
V S I G N O R A N C E R H O S G S R S T
I D G U P D H T O D V E O P D C T B D P
O F N Y H F U Y A T E Y V A F O Y I F L
U G O U S T I N C R R G E I N N U T G A
S H R I D H M I D H E I R D H F I Y H U
O J A B S O R A F J N J F F J R J F J S
R K N P R O N O R T T O N A T O B G K X
H L C N H L E N H E E N H H L N N H L B
J Q E M J Q T A U T D O R I T T M J B L
L W J Q L W Q L W Y Q L L W Y Q L U E
Z A R E P U B L I C K F Z Z S U F T J R
X E M J X M R I N C P O B T U R E X N M
W R Q F C R Q C P R O P H T R Q C C R P
```

awaken	republic	confront	irreverent
oblivious	proper	ignorance	establish

Vocabulary

● Match each word to the correct meaning.

1. communism · 피로

2. rebellious · 실패

3. failure · 공산주의

4. self-righteous · 왕조

5. battle · 허락하다

6. fatigue · 반항적인

7. impressed · 전투

8. humiliate · 놀라운

9. kneel · 독선적인

10. permit · 굴욕감을 주다

11. extraordinary · 감동을 받은

12. dynasty · 무릎을 꿇다

Lesson 3 — Guess What?

● Guess what he said in the blank.

Haven't you learned enough already? Why does a farmer need to know science and history? Do you know how much money I've already spent on you to study?

Money! Money! Money! Please stop talking about money!

You ungrateful boy!

However, Mao Zedong's fascination with the outside world did not lessen.

You pathetic boy! Far be it for you to want to help out your family as soon as possible by making some money.

East Asia Map

1. Do you know where China is on the map?

2. Can you find Korea?

3. Find other East Asian countries and write their names on the map.

4. Then color them as you like.

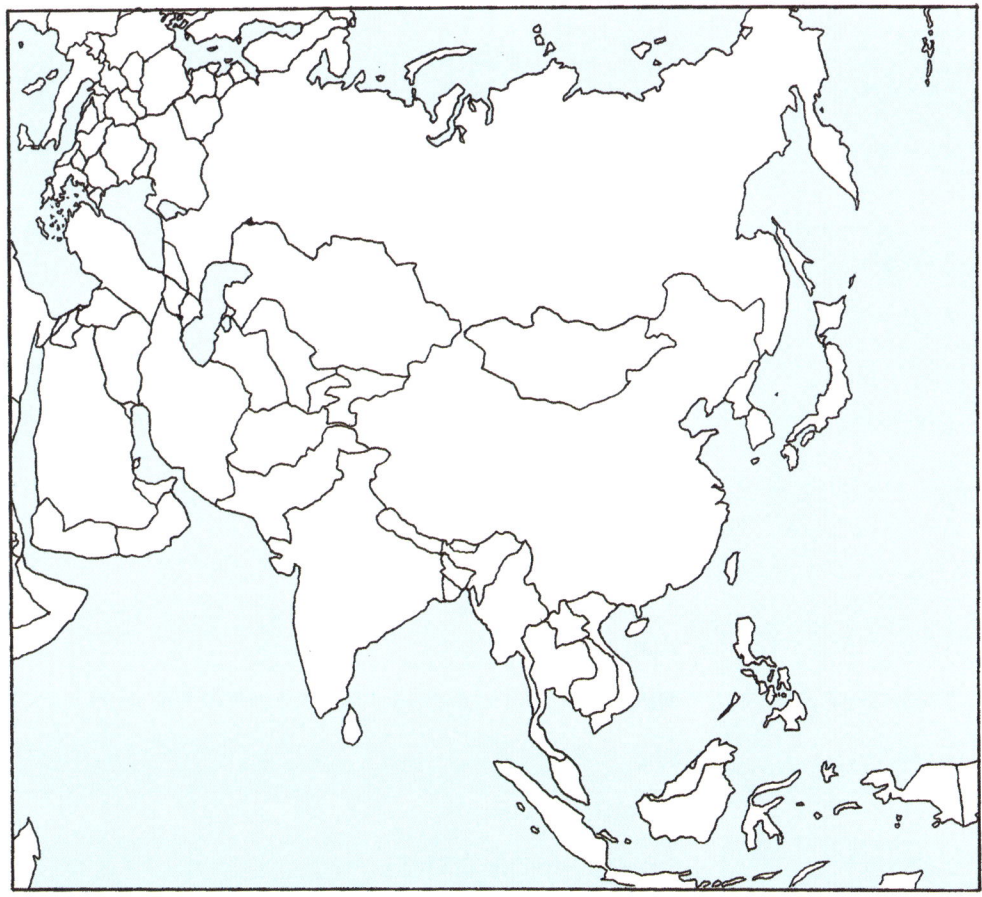

Timeline of Chinese History

2000-1500 B.C.	**Xia** 하(夏)
1700-1027 B.C.	**Shang** 상(商: '은나라'라고도 함.)
1027 - 771 B.C	**Zhou** 주(周: '서주'라고도 함.)
770 - 476 B.C.	**Spring and Autumn Period** 춘추 시대(春秋時代)
475 - 221 B.C.	**Warring States Period** 전국 시대(戰國時代)
221- 207 B.C.	**Qin** 진(秦)
206 B.C - A.D. 9	**Western Han** 서한(西漢)
9 - 24	**Xin** 신(新)
25 - 220	**Eastern Han** 동한(東漢)
220- 280	**Three Kingdoms** 삼국(三國: 위, 촉, 오)
265 - 316	**Western Jin** 서진(西晉)
317 - 420	**Eastern Jin** 동진(東晋)
420 - 588	**Southern and Northern Dynasties** 남북조(南北朝)
581 - 617	**Sui** 수(隋)
618 - 907	**Tang** 당(唐)
907 - 960	**Five Dynasties** 오대십국(五代十國)
907 - 979	**Ten Kingdoms** 오대십국(五代十國)
960- 1279	**Song** 송(宋)
1279 - 1368	**Yuan** 원(元)
1368 - 1644	**Ming** 명(明)
1644- 1911	**Qing** 청(淸)
1911 - 1949	**Republic of China** 중화민국(中華民國)
1949 -	**People's Republic of China** 중화인민공화국(中華人民共和國)

청나라 말기의 권력자, 서태후

청나라의 제12대 황제이자
마지막 황제인 푸이

청나라를 세운 누르하치

중화민국(타이완)의 위성사진

중화민국의 국기

청나라의 국기

중화 인민 공화국의 국기인 오성홍기

만리장성 ©Samxli

1893년		12월 26일, 중국 후난성 사오산 마을에서 태어납니다.
1901년	8세	학교에 입학하여 공부를 시작합니다.
1906년	13세	아버지의 강요로 학업을 중단하고 농사일을 돕습니다.
1911년	18세	군에 들어가 6개월을 복무합니다. 청나라를 무너뜨리기 위한 신해혁명에 가담합니다.
1913년	20세	후난 제1 사범 학교에 입학하여 선생님이 될 준비를 합니다.
1919년	26세	베이징 대학 도서관에서 일하며 공산주의자들을 만납니다. 창사에서 학생과 노동자 중심의 단체를 결성하여 시위를 주도합니다.
1920년	27세	잡지 「상강평론」을 창간했지만 폐간됩니다. 후난 사범 학교의 교장으로 취임합니다.
1921년	28세	제1차 중국 공산당 회의가 열립니다.
1923년	30세	공산당과 국민당이 연합합니다.
1925년	32세	국민당 대표인 쑨원이 죽습니다.
1926년	33세	고향으로 돌아가 농민들에게서 가능성을 발견합니다.

1927년 34세	국민당이 연합을 깨고 공산당을 공격하여 큰 피해를 입습니다. 농민들을 이끌고 징강산으로 피신합니다.
1931년 38세	공산당의 다른 부대와 연합하여 국민당 군대와 전쟁을 치릅니다.
1933년 40세	중국 공산당 중앙 정치국 위원에 당선됩니다.
1935년 42세	공산당 군대와 농민들과 함께 1만 킬로미터를 걸어 이동하는 '대장정'을 성공적으로 이끕니다.
1942년 49세	공산당의 지도권을 잡고 권력을 강화합니다.
1945년 52세	미국의 중재로 국민당과 화해를 시도하지만 실패합니다. 국민당과 공산당의 내전이 일어납니다.
1949년 56세	국민당과 싸움에서 승리를 거둡니다. 10월 1일, 중화 인민 공화국 정부 수립을 선포하고 주석으로 취임합니다.
1958년 65세	경제를 발전시키기 위해 '대약진 운동'을 실시합니다.
1966년 73세	권력을 강화하기 위해 반대파를 제거하는 '문화 대혁명'을 일으킵니다.
1976년 86세	9월 9일, 사망합니다.

Note

Biography Comic who?

who? 01	Barack Obama	979-11-5639-023-7
who? 02	Charles Darwin	979-11-5639-024-4
who? 03	Bill Gates	979-11-5639-025-1
who? 04	Hillary Clinton	979-11-5639-026-8
who? 05	Stephen Hawking	979-11-5639-027-5
who? 06	Oprah Winfrey	979-11-5639-028-2
who? 07	Steven Spielberg	979-11-5639-029-9
who? 08	Thomas Edison	979-11-5639-030-5
who? 09	Abraham Lincoln	979-11-5639-031-2
who? 10	Martin Luther King, Jr.	979-11-5639-032-9
who? 11	Louis Braille	979-11-5639-033-6
who? 12	Albert Einstein	979-11-5639-034-3
who? 13	Jane Goodall	979-11-5639-035-0
who? 14	Walt Disney	979-11-5639-036-7
who? 15	Winston Churchill	979-11-5639-037-4
who? 16	Warren Buffett	979-11-5639-008-4
who? 17	Nelson Mandela	979-11-5639-009-1
who? 18	Steve Jobs	979-11-5639-010-7
who? 19	J. K. Rowling	979-11-5639-011-4
who? 20	Jean-Henri Fabre	979-11-5639-012-1
who? 21	Vincent van Gogh	979-11-5639-013-8
who? 22	Marie Curie	979-11-5639-014-5
who? 23	Henry David Thoreau	979-11-5639-015-2
who? 24	Andrew Carnegie	979-11-5639-016-9
who? 25	Coco Chanel	979-11-5639-017-6
who? 26	Charlie Chaplin	979-11-5639-018-3
who? 27	Ho Chi Minh	979-11-5639-019-0
who? 28	Ludwig van Beethoven	979-11-5639-020-6
who? 29	Mao Zedong	979-11-5639-021-3
who? 30	Kim Dae-jung	979-11-5639-022-0